for you, love

Ronne Rock and Courtney Nowakowski

English Standard Version (ESV)
The Message (MSG)
New Living Translation (NLT)
Contemporary English Version (CEV)
New International Version (NIV)

for you, love ©2017

Dedication

To all the ones who have encouraged us to let our gifts take flight.

Because of you, we soar.

for you, love ©2017

About *for you, love*

For almost a decade now, my mornings have begun with Guatemalan coffee and bit of personal liturgy.

There's always a prayer — a simple and honest, "Please help me calm down and focus…" prayer that is essential for a creative girl with high-functioning anxiety and an affection for shiny objects.

Then it's time for scripture. I'll read a section — and reread it — and even listen to it, if possible. Now, I don't just read one translation. In fact, thanks to examen.me and BibleGateway.com, you'll find five on my computer screen at the same time.

English Standard Version (ESV)
The Message (MSG)
New Living Translation (NLT)
Contemporary English Version (CEV)
New International Version (NIV)

There's something about being able to read the same words in different ways that helps me find deeper meaning and perhaps even a spark of new even in old familiar passages. Now, when I first started studying scripture in this way, I would read, write a paraphrase of what was found in scripture, and take notes of what that scripture was saying to me. A second prayer would follow.

But something happened.

Over time, my prayers shifted from "help me focus on what I am reading" to "help me focus on what You, God, want me to see in the words." And the notes I've written have also shifted — they've transformed into reminders, encouragements, words I might write to someone to share what the scriptures I'm reading are teaching me about God's character, His attributes, His love. I still study scripture, still dive deep and take notes on what is moving my heart about what I'm reading, still finish with prayers to take what I've read and let it sink deeply into my heart so that my hands and feet move in time. But the paraphrases? They have become more like love notes I might send to you to share the themes found inside chapter and verse.

I always thought these "love notes" would stay in a journal. But on a plane from Guatemala to the United States, my best friend Courtney challenged us both to make a "live list" — a list of things we wanted to live in a single year. I've got my adventure list (also known as a bucket list) but, for some reason, I have never written down a "this year, I want to…" list. I'm so quick to qualify my goals — to start soaring and then start critiquing. And then I stop moving forward because I think, "those steps aren't profitable." There is wisdom — and then there is fear masked as good judgment. Far too often, I allow that fear to keep me from doing things like making New Year's resolutions and going public with big timelines and such. But at 30,000 feet, rather than allow that fear to overtake me, I looked at her and said, "OK."

She handed me paper and colored pens, and we both began writing whatever came to mind. On my list, there were things about relationships and habits and investing time in really learning Spanish. There were notes about pitching stories to publications and finishing my book, Building Eden, no matter the outcome. And then, I saw myself write down "share love notes from the Epistles, and have my best friend illustrate them." The words both terrified me and made my heart dance a little. I looked at Courtney and shared with her what I had written. She smiled. I wrote, "work with Ronne on a special project that helps others." We laughed, and **for you, love** was born. The proceeds from this book will be used to help folks who want to care for orphans and vulnerable children have that opportunity. So, when you buy this little prayer journal, know that you're also answering the prayers of people who long to serve kids. I look forward to the day when I get to write stories about those people.

So here we are now. The words once found only in my journal or in a text to a friend are now **for you, love**. The 20 love notes and contemplative images of this first volume of **for you, love** are inspired by the themes of Galatians, Ephesians, Philippians, and Colossians. Read them the way you'd read a note from a close friend. Let them encourage you to discover what He wants you to see in scripture. Write your own love notes in the spaces on the pages, and share them with someone else who needs to be reminded that God loves and He redeems and He has created us for community. The images are Courtney's response to the scriptures and to the love notes that have been born from them. Her prayer is that you'll let them be the starting place for your own response. Grab crayons or markers or pencils and make them your own. Let the accompanying scripture inspire you to not only read but also listen to what God wants to say to you. I bet He has a love note waiting. He's faithful that way.

Oh, and by the way, we've added a little something extra — five notes from Psalms. They're written just a little differently — more word painting than a love note. We thought you might like them too. Be sure to send a note or picture our way at hello@wordpainters.com so we can see what you do with the pages that follow.

Remember, we're in this together, and I am for you, love.

for you, love ©2017

About Ronne

As a writer and a lover of Jesus Christ, I find myself in awe every time I read scripture. God is a fascinating creator of story. He's truly brilliant, when you think about it. The Bible is full of plot twists, romance, mystery — things that make you cheer and things that make you rage. Even mundane passages are purposeful and rich in meaning. His words inspire me to tell stories that change stories.

An Oklahoma gal by birth, I am now situated in the Lone Star State, along with my husband Brad, son Ian, daughter-in-love Gina, and amazing grandkids Sawyer and Tyler. While the Texas Hill Country may be where I hang my hat, home for me is anywhere my heart finds its beat.

And my heart finds its strongest beat where beauty and pain collide — because hope always finds a way to peek through the cracks. There's more than 30 years of marketing and communications experience in my bones, working in television and for major corporations, global nonprofits, and multi-site churches, and I do find great joy in sharing whatever wisdom I have gained along the way. But these days, you'll more often than not find me with the vulnerable, gathering words and images that inspire others to action. I manage social media content and feature stories for Orphan Outreach, and am a multi-media journalist for Mission Network News. I'm a writer, blogger, and speaker — sharing battle-tested wisdom about leadership, advocacy marketing, and finding God in the brightest and darkest of circumstances. In addition to the *for you, love*, I'm writing **Building Eden**, a book about women who believe restoration is a reality, on earth as it is in Heaven.

About Courtney

I don't remember a time in my life when there wasn't a paintbrush or pen in my hand. God's palette is so vibrant and wonderful, and there is nothing like worshipping Him through designs that bring to life His power, His honor, His creativity, and His relentless love for each of us.

My favorite days are ones that find me covered in paint or dripping in sweat as the result of saying 'yes' to a new adventure. My husband calls me a "project sniper," because I am at my best when chaos abounds all around me, and there is nothing that I find more delightful than helping transform that chaos into calm through the power of creativity. Turning ideas into tangible things helps me feel connected to my precious Lord — no matter where He sends me.

I live in Austin, Texas, with my husband and our 19-year old daughter. Together, we serve the vulnerable in our home town. And they cheer me on as I serve orphans and at-risk children in other countries. I have found a special home in places marked for ruin — because it's there I see mercy and grace wash like watercolor to resurrect hearts and lives.

I'm honored to serve as the mission leader for NorthEast Community Church in Pflugerville, Texas. And I'm humbled to be a freelance artist and designer — God has truly given me the desires of my heart.

Our Very Many Thanks

We go into this fully expecting to fail miserably in our attempt to thank the people who have covered us in prayer, celebrated our small steps, lifted our heads when we could only see the floor, read and re-read every single word, looked at every illustration and asked the questions that needed to be asked, and most of all, have been our faithful friends. We're going to give it our best shot, and ask your forgiveness in advance if we missed you in our eagerness to send this page to our wonderful (and patient) book designer, Scott Cuzzo.

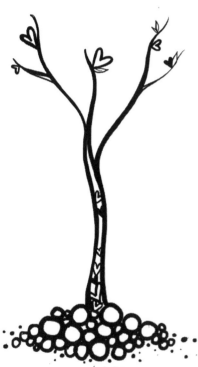

First of all, we want to thank Diane Zimmerman. We met her as part of the TinyTribe of folks who send encouragement on a regular basis. She said, "yes" to reading the rough draft, and then provided us with thoughtful and gracious edits that were precise and purposeful. She invested herself in the book as a labor of love, and her work made us better. Next, we are over-the-moon thankful for our brother, David Bouchard. We are kin in a powerful way. He's listened to our tearful confessions of inadequacy and reminded us of our broken beauty and calling. He, along with Amy Warr, who we describe as "the presence," are our safe harbor. We are dreaming with them right now about a project that will give voice to the vulnerable in a beautiful way. Elora Ramirez, you saw the story before we saw the story — thank you. Our gratitude to the Beta-Beauties (the 11+1) who agreed to read our words and look at our images and let us know if any of them mattered. And wow — thanks to Kristy Simpson. You may never know her name, but you likely feel the impact of her prayers.

From Courtney — Hey you — yep, you Vero, my god-crafted sister, thank you for reminding me that my lines and squiggles have kingdom purpose and not letting up until I acknowledged it too. Thank you, Mom and Dad, for teaching me to try. Thank you, sweet S.Now, for being so passionate about sharing His story. And thank you, my beloved Ryan Nowakowski, for the gifts of electronic art supplies, daily doses of laughter, buying in to a life of pouring out, and for the million ways you encourage me to fly.

From Ronne — Thank you, Bradley K, for finding your joy in me finding mine. This girl who loves words can't find enough of them to express her love for you. Thank you to the bigs and the littles for continuing to inspire me with your love for each other and for our God. Hey Sawyer, we will always be "word people." Thank you to Melissa for fighting for me when I wanted to not fight at all. Thank you, Sarah, for quietly asking about the stories. Thank you, Kellye, for letting me be raw. BabyBird2 — my Charlene — you have been cheering for years, and it brings tears to my eyes. And oh my gosh, Courtney. There's a reason you are my best friend. You know me and yet you love me. Fully. I can't ask for more than that.

for you, love ©2017.

8

How we Hope You'll enjoy THIS BOOK:

breathe You're not being timed or graded. Instead we invite you to read the words, interact with the illustrations and ponder what He's saying to you.

journey There are ~~rules~~. You don't have to use this ~~book~~ every day. You can read it out of order. Just use it. We simply want you to take hold of the opportunity to hear what God says about you as His **beloved** creation. Our hope is that this book will be a restorative journey for your ♥. That by spending time with Him you'll truly believe that you are not the exception to god's love. You are greatly loved.

share We want to know what God is teaching you! Share with us at HELLO@WORDPAINTERS.COM

To You. For You. Because of You.

Inspired by verses in Galatians 1

Let God's curse fall on anyone, including us or even an angel from heaven, who preaches a different kind of Good News than the one we preached to you. I say again what we have said before: If anyone preaches any other Good News than the one you welcomed, let that person be cursed. Galatians 1:8–9 NLT

Prayer: Your words are enough to me, God. Your love notes are enough for me. You are complete, and I am complete in You. Please help me remember that, when life wants to rip apart Your words and call them not enough. Please help me remember that, when the weight of "kill, steal, and destroy" threatens to crush everything in its path. Please keep my eyes open to see You moving the walls back to reveal eternity. Please let me not forget that Your joy is in writing love notes not only to me but through me, so that others may know Your great love and find themselves complete in You.

beautiful one DON'T LISTEN TO THE ONES WHO SAY love notes ARE FOR FAIRYTALES they are for you

for you, love ©2017

This is a love note. To you, beautiful one. Because you are worthy of every word ever written about what love is and what love does and what love finds you to be.

This is a love note to you, written by God.

Yes, the God who spoke existence and shaped life finds His joy in taking words and moving them about like paint on a canvas, just for you. He pours into humanity and reveals His embrace through aging hands and clumsy feet and smiles that tilt slightly to the left. He speaks in accents and lisps and eloquence and song.

His words. To you. For you. Because of you.

Read them. Cherish them. Believe them.

Don't let anyone edit them with bleeding ink that mars their beauty or diminishes their worth. Don't let anyone attempt to tear them like tissue. Don't listen to the ones who say love notes are for fairy tales.

This is a love note to you, beautiful one — a love note written by God. Read it now, and carry it with you always.

"From before time found its way to moments, you have been My delight. My joy is in moving back the walls of this world for you so that you may see the eternity in the days that I've placed in your heart. You are royalty and warrior and majesty and ministry, and all of heaven cheers when you see a kingdom in your midst and a crown on your head. Oh love, I am here for you always — every day mercies new. I am complete, and you are complete in Me."

Is Enough

Inspired by verses in Galatians 2

For through the law I died to the law, so that I might live to God. I have been crucified with Christ. It is no longer I who live, but Christ who lives in me. And the life I now live in the flesh I live by faith in the Son of God, who loved me and gave Himself for me. I do not nullify the grace of God, for if righteousness were through the law,then Christ died for no purpose. Galatians 2:19–21 ESV

Prayer: I am holding tightly to this one thought today, "This love is enough for my welcome." The love that knows me best and knows me longest and knows me most is the love that is always enough to cover every good and hard piece of me. It's the love that covers me in dignity. It's the love that clothes me in royalty. It's the love that says, "creatively made for this very moment." Your love, oh great God, is small enough to hear me and large enough to hold me. Always enough, always enough.

for you, love ©2017

You know I love to talk about you, to tell others about you, to join all heaven in singing songs about you. And if I do, consider how much our great God loves to talk about you too.

But these words will never be uttered from His mouth as He woos you with His kindness.

"Love isn't enough for your welcome."

The deafening noise of more will always be there. It will taunt you with lists and tug at your soul with laws. More wants to keep you cowering, afraid of being found illegitimate when all others wear the family crest. More stabs at your heart and laughs as it bleeds. More tells you there will never be enough time, never enough understanding, never enough obedience, never enough you.

Don't listen to more. Instead, remember this.

"This love is enough for your welcome."

Love shaped like crucible. Love drawn from the depths. Love that embosses us with a dove and seals us with fire. Love that marks boundaries of mercy and hope and as far as east is to the west. Love that is the more — always the more — forever the more. Love that pours out the immeasurably more like water, love that lets you splash in its reservoirs of grace.

This, dear one, is what God is saying about you. "My love is enough."

Wake Up, Love

Inspired by verses in Galatians 3

You foolish Galatians! Who has bewitched you? Before your very eyes Jesus Christ was clearly portrayed as crucified. I would like to learn just one thing from you: Did you receive the Spirit by the works of the law,or by believing what you heard? Are you so foolish? After beginning by means of the Spirit, are you now trying to finish by means of the flesh? Have you experienced so much in vain — if it really was in vain? So again I ask, does God give you his Spirit and work miracles among you by the works of the law, or by your believing what you heard?
Galatians 3:1–5 NIV

Wake up because the day awaits you and:

Prayer: Oh kind God, I need You to lean in close so I can match Your rhythmic breathing, so my heart will slow. You have not abandoned me, You have not forsaken me. I am not an exception — rather, I am exceptional in Your eyes. Give me eyes to see that. Give me eyes to see You now.

Wake up, love. You were having a nightmare. You were running in your sleep, running so hard. Look at the sheets, the blanket, your hair — twisted, braided, damp from the salty drops of fear that consumed you, possessed you.

Open up your eyes love, and see the day breaking through the darkness. It's been waiting for you, always waiting for you. Even as night falls and the shadows grow, day is there leaving reminders scattered in the sky, glowing scarlet and cerulean and freshwater pearl. Day is there always to transform salty drops into crystal.

Day has transformed you, love. It has warmed you and calmed you and walked with you. Day has not left you even now. Even when the nightmares scream that the day is inadequate to keep you in its presence and twist your soul into running.

You will run straight into Day. Because it has you now.

Day awaits you. So wake up, love. Wake up and rise up and wear crystals that proclaim your transformation. Let the light reflect and gleam.

Ink on Your Heart

Inspired by verses in Galatians 4

But when the time arrived that was set by God the Father, God sent His Son, born among us of a woman, born under the conditions of the law so that He might redeem those of us who have been kidnapped by the law. Thus we have been set free to experience our rightful heritage. You can tell for sure that you are now fully adopted as His own children because God sent the Spirit of His Son into our lives crying out, "Papa! Father!" Doesn't that privilege of intimate conversation with God make it plain that you are not a slave, but a child? And if you are a child, you're also an heir, with complete access to the inheritance. Galatians 4:4–7 MSG

Prayer: I sit here in the quiet and close my eyes, Lord. And I see Your hands with my name written. It's right there, on Your palm. It's there, never-fading, never-running, never-washing away. My name. My heart. The penmanship is the same. It's Yours. The crimson ink is Yours. The belonging is Yours. The liberty — Yours. I am daisy and I am puddle and I am words. And I am in awe.

for you, love ©2017

Remember the days when you were so small, the days when treasure was collected in piggy banks and glass jars — saved for wonder that was so far from reach by little hands? Remember when freedom was staying up late or the excitement of a snow day or the joy of a report card reward? Remember all the "when I grow up, I'll..." bold statements of always and never and different?

Remember when treasure became more, and freedom became real, and you looked in the mirror and realized grown up was now?

And you looked at the face staring back at you and said, "I certainly can't be trusted. I still feel so small."

Oh, how I wish I could help you now see how precious liberty really is, and that the true liberty you long for can't be found in pennies or attaboy rewards. Liberty is held out for you in hands that hold time itself. Liberty is held out for you in hands stained with the crimson ink bearing the manifesto of your freedom — the same ink that has been written across your heart, "Belongs to God."

True liberty is for you, it is your treasure and your snow day and all the everythings you've longed for time and time again. Don't hide from it, love. Don't be afraid. Don't look at the ink on your heart and say, "Three words aren't enough words. Surely I can't be trusted with the wonder of just three words. I'll find more words to add. I'll collect words now. I'll write all the words to make the liberty small {because I still feel so small}."

Don't be afraid of the words and the ink. This is true liberty. You are not small in it. You are appropriately placed. You are the very lifeblood of the Almighty. He ties you to Himself in affection. His belonging is His promise and His purpose. He has created you. Like daisies belong to flowers and puddles belong to water, you are His image and His likeness.

Crimson ink writes your true liberty. "Belongs to God" is enough for you today and all the todays.

Emancipation

Inspired by verses in Galatians 5

Christ has set us free to live a free life. So take your stand! Never again let anyone put a harness of slavery on you. It is absolutely clear that God has called you to a free life. Just make sure that you don't use this freedom as an excuse to do whatever you want to do and destroy your freedom. Rather, use your freedom to serve one another in love; that's how freedom grows. For everything we know about God's Word is summed up in a single sentence: Love others as you love yourself. That's an act of true freedom.
Galatians 5:13–14 MSG

Prayer: I want to be free, Jesus. Oh, yes. I do want to be free. I will repeat the words, "I am free. I am free. I am free." until the vibration of my voice moves from my head to my heart. I will not sway to the song of captivity and I will not step in time to a dirge. I am alive, I am unshackled. I will repeat the words, "I am free. I am free. I am free." I am grabbing Your hand and moving now. I want to be free. I am free.

for you, love ©2017

Chains are broken on the fence that holds you in. You are free, love.

Free.

Free to step off gravel and on to grass. Free to step out of shadow and into sun. Free to shed the blaze that calls you out as prisoner and put on the brilliance that calls you out as prized.

So step out. Don't let the liberty frighten you back into the cage. Don't allow the voices behind you to cause your head to turn. You are free, love. Free from slavery, free from bondage, free from the stench of latrines and dirty laundry. You are no longer bound. Step all the way out, not just one foot in freedom while your soul remains tied. Don't let the ghost of the shackles weigh you down. Ghosts bear down hard sometimes. But you are not dead. You are alive. And you are free.

He's done that for you. Christ has done that because of you. He has spoken, and chains fall at His voice. He has opened the gate with a glance. He has stepped inside the cage and looked you in the eye. And He has said, "Emancipation."

So step now. Embrace love now. Let the brilliance you wear be a warm light for those still dressed in blaze. Don't let it blind others or burn them or make them fall back into the prison cage.

Step now. Let go of the ghosts now — no more soul-selling or heart-breaking or tearing down and tearing apart. Emancipation. He looked at you and said, "Emancipation." Step now, and don't step back.

Step out and let brilliance do its work in you, through you, warming the world around you. Christ's emancipation shines in your love and your kindness and your gentle way of staying and keeping. You are free. Nothing can hold you now. Ghosts are gone. It's time to shine.

Hands Like Braids

Inspired by verses in Galatians 6

Bear one another's burdens, and so fulfill the law of Christ. For if anyone thinks he is something, when he is nothing, he deceives himself. But let each one test his own work, and then his reason to boast will be in himself alone and not in his neighbor. For each will have to bear his own load. Let the one who is taught the word share all good things with the one who teaches. Galatians 6:2–6 ESV

Prayer: Precious Father, may I feel the warmth and weight of Your hands at this moment? May I feel the tenderness of You reaching out to catch a finger and another and another in tender affirmation that You are here and You are not fleeing and my hands are not too small or too large or too calloused for You? And Father, will You forgive me all the times I have looked but have not touched the hand you've whispered, "hold." We are frail without touch. We fall without touch. Father, I don't want ground to be our destiny when we are meant to soar.

for you, love ©2017

Here they are. My hands. Here they are for you. I know they bear the scars of days gone by, and they aren't soft anymore — the callouses of years and struggles and mistakes are embossed on them like brands on cowhide. But here they are for you. You're standing now, we're standing now. And I want us to stay standing. So my hands, they are for you to hold you up and hold you together. To hold us together, because He has designed our hands to link like braids. He does that so He may fit himself in their midst. He holds our hands together.

Together, our hands do good for others. They are here to reach and to cradle, to move and sway and carry. We dig with them, dive with them, find life with them. We till the ground and sow down deep. And life is given life when we present our hands to each other as gifts. We will not grow tired, love. We will not grow weary. We will do good with our hands.

And we will hold them up as shields to defend against the darkness, against the ones who say love alone is inadequate and the cross is a broken sword. They don't need to be beaten down — they need to be reminded of what your hands represent. You are an image-bearer of the One who is enough, you are an ambassador of love that is enough, you are a warrior of grace upon grace upon grace. Your hands are mercy, your hands are justice, your hands are hope. Your hands are made new, always new. With scars and callouses and marks that bear your story, your hands tell His story. My hands tell His story. And our story is for each other.

And we link like braids.

Champagne and Confetti

Inspired by verses in Ephesians 1

Long before He laid down earth's foundations, He had us in mind, had settled on us as the focus of His love, to be made whole and holy by His love. Ephesians 1:4 MSG

made whole & holy

Prayer: You call me a saint. You, God All-Mighty, call me a saint. When I am trapped in the mire of my own making, You call me a saint. When I am weary of endless days chilled to the bone, You call me a saint. When I am blazing for You and all feels like heaven's gate, You call me a saint. You celebrate me with champagne and confetti and You tell me, "Gather others. Gather My people now." I am not an afterthought or an alternative. You call me saint. That overwhelms me. I am undone in its beauty. You say You are right there, ready to reveal Your purpose, ready to reveal Your plan. You have so much to share with me — glimpses into stories not yet told, stories of rescue and stories of hope. Stories You say have my name written in, stories You say have a place for my prayers and obedience. Sweet Jesus, please give me Your strength to walk in faith and in wisdom and boundless love. May I see myself through Your brilliance today? May I see myself as resplendent and always new? May I honor You in my steps today — may they be the steps of a saint who glories in her divine heritage, who sees such worth in her inheritance, who finds herself humbly serving with gratitude the Creator of saints?

saint → someone with an exceptional degree of holiness or closeness to God

for you, love ©2017

You are a saint.

Let's start there. You, loved one, are a saint — named that by the very God who created you to be His own. You will not be found on a charm, and your name won't be found in prayer books. But let this not escape you. You are a saint. Grace and peace are yours — given to you by your Lord.

Oh, how God deserves such praise for what He has provided through the life of Jesus Christ. His most holy gifts overflow for you, designed for you before time made its mark and this world became our home. Rewind now to before the beginning, before life and birth and striving and falling and paradise and that Voice speaking "it is good." Before anything began, the conversation included you. You as orphan no more, you as child with legacy, you as beautiful beyond measure. You as stumbling, learning to walk, learning to run, learning to dance, learning to be still and be embraced heir of Kingdom of Heaven. That moment could not wait to celebrate this moment, with grace poured out like champagne and love falling down like confetti. You have the DNA of divinity in your veins, redeeming even the most fragile parts of you. You are forgiven for every forgotten kindness and intentional hardship and for lifting high your life rather than laying it down for a life so beautiful. You are welcomed in to the conversation now, listening intently as "this is My will — this is My good pleasure" is spoken. You get to see His desire to gather. Oh, God loves to gather His people. All creation sings when His people are gathered.

He is gathering now, and He says, "You, saint, will help. Share the champagne and confetti with another now."

And you are His people. His lineage. You are the photo He shows with a smile. You are the stories He tells. He holds out His inheritance — an inheritance filled with hope and glory. He puts a ring on your finger and says "this one — My own." He gives you a wax seal for every moment, and stamps it the signet of "leading to holiness." He is there when in darkness you snap the seal, to repair and restore. He will not allow the seal to bear another mark — He will keep you even when you are not keeping Him.

Because you were in His heart before time became time. And so every day is filled with new mercies for you. Every day is filled with amazing grace for you. Every moment is filled with divinity for you.

You, the saint.

And so I give thanks for you. I give thanks for your life and your faith and the story that's being written in and through you. I give thanks that I get to pray bold prayers for you — prayers for your present and prayers for your future, prayers for wisdom and discernment and understanding, prayers for your eyes be able to take in all that He has prepared for you. Both for this life and for eternity. I pray you are refreshed by His power that knows no limits and restored by His love that is boundless. I pray you see yourself as you are seen through the brilliance of Jesus. Radiant, resplendent, always new. He is Lord, He is King, He is Ruler, He is Head. And you, saint, are complete in Him.

Autographed by God

Inspired by verses in Ephesians 2

But God is so rich in mercy, and He loved us so much, that even though we were dead because of our sins, He gave us life when He raised Christ from the dead. ~ God saved you by His grace when you believed. And you can't take credit for this; it is a gift from God. Salvation is not a reward for the good things we have done, so none of us can boast about it. For we are God's masterpiece. He has created us anew in Christ Jesus, so we can do the good things He planned for us long ago. Ephesians 2:4–5, 9–10 NLT

Prayer: What an artist You are, God. You take crumbling ruins and broken tombstones and create castles and galleries. You make bold brushstrokes of mercy and paint the finest of detail in love and hope and forgiveness. You paint in hues that become brighter with the days, revealing ever-new shades. There is no flaw in Your work, no cracks over time. Every design reveals time and timelessness. Every design reveals Your personality. Every design has Your signature. Today, would You let me catch a glimpse of the colors You have painted? Would You help my eyes to see the beauty of every single design, to find value in each person who has been autographed by You? Father, I want to stand in awe of what You have done when I see people who have been washed in color by Christ's redeeming love. And I want to carry the color into the graveyard and gray, joyfully showing the words "welcome here" and "hope-full" and "no longer alone."

We are grace-full remnants, love. We are scraps filled with majesty and wonder of the Almighty. Our poverty is overwhelmed by His wealth. He gives us life. He makes us beautiful. He takes little beggars like us and makes us worthy. XO

for you, love ©2017

Stop and remember. Remember the days before these days, remember the days when everything around us was graveyard and gray. Remember the days of talking big and fearing bigger — of staking claims on land that crumbled like dust. We thought we knew it all then, thought if we just tried a little harder and walked a little taller and acted a little smarter, we would certainly make it. But we were trapped in graveyard and gray. Then, with paintbrush laden, we were washed with color. Crimson gave way to gleaming. The grass grew soft under our feet and the gnarled trees bloomed. Graveyard became garden — new mercies and grace springing up all around us. Extravagant love did that for us — even as we stumbled breathless in the gray — God's perfect pouring out love painted "new" on our hearts and souls. He made us living masterpieces in Christ, perfect pictures of His affection. He painted color we could never have mixed. He designed the life we could have never created. He drew the lines and painted every highlight and shadow — He selected the palette and chose the brushstrokes to make us beautiful, to make us purposeful. And He hand-signed His work.

We are autographed by God. And we are made to reflect His artistry.

What a precious thought — that He would see beyond our dusty gray stumbling and say we are worthy of a museum, that He would look at us and say "prized." The paints God used on us — listen to their names! There is "hope-full" and "no longer alone." There is "peace" and there is "no more hatred." There is "reconcile" and there is "welcome here." And the brush carries its own name — Jesus. He makes us magnificent, He makes us His own. We are autographed by God. And He displays us so all can see our beautiful colors and read the names — and feel the brushstrokes on graveyard and gray.

Knees become Roots.

Inspired by verses in Ephesians 3

When I think of all this, I fall to my knees and pray to the Father, the Creator of everything in heaven and on earth. I pray that from His glorious, unlimited resources He will empower you with inner strength through His Spirit. Then Christ will make His home in your hearts as you trust in Him. Your roots will grow down into God's love and keep you strong. Ephesians 3:14–17 NLT

Prayer: Oh God of the garden, I am overwhelmed to think that You would see me as a Christ-tree, that You would graft me in to eternity and let me be part of giving eternity's hope to those who are hungry and thirsty and in need of shade. Oh sweet Father, don't let my knees grow weary — for it's in humbling myself in communion that You transform my kneeling to growing, my weakness to strength. It's in the garden with You that I taste love — love that wants to be shared with others. I can't love well without You. Lord, let me not want to close the gates to anyone. Let my branches dance in celebration for every hesitant soul who hears Your voice.

for you, love ©2017

Close your eyes, little love. Close your eyes and imagine a garden. It's there behind a gleaming gate held up by — wait, it stands on its own. The gate swings wide for you. You look down and see the invitation in your hand.

"Taste and see."

But I'm not a gardner, you say. I shall surely destroy the beauty — I am not trained, I am not equipped, I am not...

And then a Voice in the garden speaks.

"Take this."

And your hand reaches out for the bloom.

"Grace is her name."

You look around, the heavens infinite above you and no horizon below. The fragrance overwhelms you, and knees grow weak. The Voice speaks again.

"Take this."

And your hand reaches out for the fruit that looks like nine.

"Life is her name. Taste her. Taste compassion and kindness, taste peace and steadfastness. Taste gentleness and joy. Taste love and discipline and always forever faithful."

You taste. And you long to put the fruit in a basket and give it to all who hunger. There are so many hungry. So many.

You fall to your knees. And knees become roots watered by tears of gratitude and adoration. Fruit in your hands becomes fruit on your limbs, ever-growing for others to receive.

You hear the Voice yet again.

"You, my love. Look at you, growing strong. You are a Christ-tree, bearing His image and His life and His love. You offer shade for parched souls. You offer refreshment for the weary. You offer shelter for the hurting. Your branches dance in celebration and in invitation."

There you are, rooted and grounded in love. There you are, tasting eternity. Glory, love. The garden gates swing wide, and you hear the familiar words in the distance. You smile.

"But I am not a gardener..."

And then the Voice.

for you, love ©2017

Long Road Together.

Inspired by verses in Ephesians 4

Then we will no longer be infants, tossed back and forth by the waves, and blown here and there by every wind of teaching and by the cunning and craftiness of people in their deceitful scheming. Instead, speaking the truth in love, we will grow to become in every respect the mature body of him who is the head, that is, Christ.
Ephesians 4:14–15 ESV

Prayer: Oh Father God, you have set our feet in beautiful places. This long road is filled with everything pertaining to a life lived richly in Your love. You have surrounded us with people to refine that love, to deepen faith, to reveal Your image. I should be always grateful, always ready to keep walking, never tempted by the sirens. And yet, I confess that there are times I would rather not walk at all. There are seasons I would rather find solace in darkness rather than find healing in light. There are moments I would rather be alone, rather not be bothered by the people who feel more like sandpaper than silk, rather hand-pick who passes the baton my way — or the person my hands reach out to help. Forgive me for not walking well. Please today, sweet Lord — clear eyes to see, nimble legs to respond, open hands ready for whatever — and whoever — You set before them. Today, Lord, let me honor You by walking well. Today, Lord, let there be an opportunity to say "we're in this together and I believe in you."

for you, love ©2017

We're walking this long road together, you and me. So let's walk it well. It's a road that winds and curves and is filled with days of storm and days of spring. Our destination is lovely, but there are moments we wonder if we'll ever get there. And so we walk. Together.

So let's be gentle with each other, let's not puff ourselves up and treat the walk as some race to be won but rather a relay where we hold each other up and pass our baton back and forth to say "we're in this and I've believe in you." Let's find no greater joy than to celebrate peace with each other as we walk. We are part of the same family, greatly loved by the same Father and bound together by the same Spirit. Hope is our heartbeat. Our Lord has gone to hell and back for us to prove His adoration of us and His desire for us to be with this family, on this road, walking this walk. And He did something else because He knew we would some days wonder if we'd ever get there. He gave each of us gifts to share. Some of us can see the destination more clearly, some of us can encourage even the most disheartened. Some of us tend to wounds and some of us know how to nourish. Oh, and there are those on the walk who call those who haven't yet started the journey, saying, "we're in this and we believe in you and please walk — please walk." And together, our gifts become the purest gift of celebration that we truly ARE in this and every step of our walk informs and builds and strengthens our faith in the God who claims us and walks with us. We walk into understanding. We walk into wholeness. He completes every small thing that concerns us as we walk. Eyes become clear and legs become strong. Hands become eager to hold and hearts become hungry for truth. And we learn to love — real, abiding, overcoming, always-present, never-shirking, going-to-the-depths love that has healing and life coursing through its veins. Love that makes us real. Love that knits us together.

That's what the walk does for us. Oh yes, let's walk it well.

You'll hear the siren call on the road, because the road is long and there are stretches that seem unending. You'll hear the sound of the calling away to darker paths, to "no one else but me" and "no time but now" and "don't give a damn." Those paths make hearts brittle and knees weak and love evaporate. Here's my hand. Hold it when the sound overwhelms you. Let me dust the darkness from your radiant clothes and sing over you to drown out the clamor.

"God the glorious, we are His own. God the glorious, His love is shown. Christ, our Lord and King, mighty in grace. Christ, our Lord and King, now face-to-face."

We are walking this long road together, you and me. Let's walk it well. Let's care for each other, disagreeing with dignity so that we give no room for division to do harm. Let's lay down entitlement and privilege, and labor well to serve others first. Let's watch our words, using each as steps to help someone climb higher and not bricks to bury them. Let's love each other the way we have been loved so richly by Christ. Let's hold each other to the highest, seeing everyone on the road as precious and valuable and worthy of great honor. Let's hold each other to the highest, praying for those who haven't yet taken a hand. Let's be kind. Let's forgive quickly. Let's be gentle.

Every day, let's say "we're in this and I believe in you."

for you, love ©2017

Soliloquy

Inspired by verses in Ephesians 5

You groped your way through that murk once, but no longer. You're out in the open now. The bright light of Christ makes your way plain. So no more stumbling around. Get on with it! The good, the right, the true — these are the actions appropriate for daylight hours. Figure out what will please Christ, and then do it. Sing songs from your heart to Christ. Sing praises over everything, any excuse for a song to God the Father in the name of our Master, Jesus Christ. Ephesians 5:8–10, 21 MSG

Prayer: Oh precious King, You spared not one small thing in the love story You have written. And this — this brings me to my knees — that Your story would have my name written in it. In ink that will not fade, on paper that will not tear, in a book that cannot burn. Your love story is light. Your love story is life. I am breathing in that life right now. Let me not forget to breathe. Let my eyes not grow weary of the pages of Your book. And let me never close my fingers around the treasure spilled out and overflowing, claiming it as mine — only mine. Keep fear distant and keep darkness at bay. Let Your love be my soliloquy, let me sing out the pages of the love story even if no one listens. Let me love with the same measure of love I have received from You, my King. Let me find room in Your crimson and cream for pauper and predator. Let me not spare one small thing in holding out Your love story in trembling hands. Love for all ages. Love for all time. That is Your love. I am breathing in again.

for you, love ©2017

This is a love story. A story for the ages. A story for all time. A story of dragon slayers and a gleaming city on a hill.

You, precious one, are the object of the King's affection. That love has stormed the very gates of hell for you. It has stripped death of its seething power for you. It has quenched the damning fires that threaten to destroy you. It has pierced the very soul of the enemy. An that love has done more. It has wrapped you in crimson and cream and given you a crown, it has given you a glorious name and called you His own, for always and forever.

And the love of the King is not love that wants to be cheered or coddled or patted on the back for its great sacrifice. No, it is a divine love that has known you as pauper and predator and still sees you as worthy.

The King sees you as worthy. Oh, that is a love to cherish. That is a love divine — a love that simply longs to see your face and hear your voice.

The King has eyes for you. Look at Him now. Look at Him and smile.

His love is treasure spilled out and overflowing. It's there now, in your hands. And then, the story takes a turn — a most awe-inspiring twist. Your hands suddenly tremble with the weight of the gifts you have received. And the King nods. "Let this love spill through you now, let it wrap everything in crimson and cream, let it become love story for paupers and predators who walk alongside you."

What a love to be given to others, this love of the King. Love that raises rather than ruins. Love that delights rather than debases. Love that lights up darkest skies and resurrects life in its warmth. You hold that love in your hands, you know. That love is diamonds in coal mines, pure and bright.

That love is song.

That love is sonnet.

That love is your soliloquy.

That love, the love that storms hell and slays dragons and destroys death and redeems paupers and predators, the love of a King who delights in your smile and your voice. That love, in your trembling hands.

You kneel and hold out that love. Love for the ages. Love for all time.

And you sing.

It's Time for Brave, Love.

Inspired by verses in Ephesians 6

Be ready! Let the truth be like a belt around your waist, and let God's justice protect you like armor. Your desire to tell the good news about peace should be like shoes on your feet. Let your faith be like a shield, and you will be able to stop all the flaming arrows of the evil one. Let God's saving power be like a helmet, and for a sword use God's message that comes from the Spirit. Never stop praying, especially for others. Always pray by the power of the Spirit. Stay alert and keep praying for God's people.
Ephesians 6:14-18 CEV

Prayer: Today, Mighty God, today let me not be reluctant in putting the armor on. Today, truth wraps itself around me, and righteousness guards my heart. Today, best-news peace echoes with every step I take. Today, salvation is not shadowed — it is celebrated. Today, faith shields me from shame, and Your very life flows through my hands as I reach into darkness to shatter it with love. Let this be my proclamation, Mighty God. Let this be my brave. Today, I will fight the battle. Today, I will wage war against the fog. Today, I will not dull the light. I will let it reflect off the sword and let it gleam from the shield. I will let it light up my steps and leave a trail of peace that glimmers like gold. I will let it powerfully work to transform lives as it cries out in battle, "You are loved and you are beautiful and your life is made to be fully alive." I will let it be radiant in me and through me. Today, Mighty God, I will be a warrior. Today, it's time for brave love.

It's time for brave, love. It's time for brave.

We're at war here — a bloody battlefield for loyalty. The accuser would love nothing more than to redirect our focus through the fog of lies and shame. His seething voice cheers when we destroy each other.

It's time for brave, love.

It's time to put on armor and stand for light. Truth wraps around you as a guard, and righteousness protects your heart. Peace covers your feet as you walk. "I am saved and I am safe" covers you. Oh, and look at the faith in your hand. Beautiful, powerful faith, drenched in the love of Christ. That dripping-in-love faith drowns destruction. You've got God Himself as the sword with which you'll destroy the wiles of every enemy. And there your battle cry of prayer. Breath prayers and written prayers and spoken prayers and prayers so deep they can't find the words. You have them. And they will change the world.

Every piece is there, waiting for you. He is giving them to you. Now.

It's time for brave, love. It's time for brave.

It's time to step and step again, it's time to speak and speak again, it's time to pray and pray again. It's time to be warrior. It's time to be army. It's time to invade darkness and illuminate every corner. It's time to rescue. It's time to destroy destruction. It's time to love relentlessly, fearlessly.

Picture Book

Inspired by verses in Philippians 1
Every time I think of you, I thank my God. And
whenever I mention you in my prayers, it
makes me happy. This is because you have
taken part with me in spreading the good
news from the first day you heard about it.
God is the one who began this good work
in you, and I am certain that
He won't stop before it is complete
on the day that Christ Jesus returns.
Philippians 1:4–6 CEV

*Prayer: Sweet Lord, let me always
remember to look at the pictures You've
taken, the pictures You've added to the
days of my life. Let me look at the stories
You continue to write without fail – the most
beautiful of all stories that could possibly be
written about this girl. You have spoken me
into creation. Let me not forget that what You've
begun in me will be faithfully fulfilled in me, because
that's how completely You love. And don't ever let me
become blind to the stories You are writing in others. Let me
cheer at every photo, cheer at every word on the page — even
when the stories are not yet known or the eyes are blind to the ash
of Your camera as You take one more picture saying, "This one is mine —
this one I adore."*

for you, love ©2017

There is a moment in my day which is one of my favorite moments of all.

It's the moment I give thanks for you, my love.

The reasons are like a picture book — image after image after image of who you are and what you mean to me. The stories are precious and real and flawed and perfect, and every story gives way to prayer that there will be so many more.

Let's add pages to the picture book. Images of laughter and of tears, of steadfast focus on roads so long. Let's add stories of coming to the rescue and standing up for good and long conversations about everything that matters and moments when no words are needed at all. Every story added to the book is a chapter in God's greater story — not one word He writes will be edited. His story begins and ends with 'I love you.' It begins and ends with Christ.

He loves us, friend. And He loves how we love.

Let's make new albums and give them away so they may be filled up with images and stories, so that love will grow and Heaven will enlarge. Let's sit with the ones struggling to see the story at all, and uncover hidden pictures of hope. Let's be patient with the ones afraid to share the images, and point out the divinity in them.

Let's be kind to the ones who deny the stories are real.

For the days you and I have here together, let's keep adding pictures. For the days we are here, let's keep giving thanks for the stories, never afraid to let them be written, always grateful for the love inside even the hardest words.

Pray You Never Forget

Inspired by verses in Philippians 2

Then make me truly happy by agreeing wholeheartedly with each other, loving one another, and working together with one mind and purpose. Don't be selfish; don't try to impress others. Be humble, thinking of others as better than yourselves. Don't look out only for your own interests, but take an interest in others, too. Philippians 2:2–4 NLT

Prayer: Sweet Jesus, please let me never forget that I am Yours — that I am made in image and likeness, that divinity flows through my veins and eternity is set in my heart. Please help me to remember that my life is hidden in Your life, and that I am here in this season to share that life fully with others. Please help me love well and love without measure. Let me be unafraid to empty myself every day, knowing that in it Your great joy is revealed.

Hey, my precious one. There's something I've wanted to tell you for so long. It's my deepest prayer for you, my greatest joy, my highest hope. The list is long of those things that I would love to wish for you — that it would always go well for you, that success would find itself your greatest fan, that the land would be expanded under every step you take, and the path would always be smooth and well-marked, that you would forever be held in honor by all who meet you, that there would never be troubled days.

I would love to wish all those things, and I do. But this — this is my deepest prayer, coming from the depths of my greatest love for you. This is the one that remains when all the candle flames turn to vapor and shooting stars disappear into dust and wishes granted reveal new longings.

I pray you never forget Whose you are, love.

You are eternity wrapped in humanity, divine DNA flowing through tiny veins, adopted into new family never to be alone again. Your name is carved into family trees and tattooed near the heart of a Creator who adores you with mother heart and cherishes you with father heart.

And you are here for more than wishes.

Look at your hands, love. They are there for the holding. Your legs are there for the carrying. Your shoulders are there for the leaning. Your ears are there for the hearing prayers unspoken, your eyes there for the seeing pain unseen. Your life is there for the giving life to others. The adoration felt for you is for the pouring out, giving away, emptying just to watch it fill and fill again.

Don't be afraid to be Whose you are. Don't be afraid.

Love well. Please love well.

He has your life in His hands. He carries you with His legs. His shoulders are broad for every day.

Your life — it will be filled, love. The love that counts will be filled again for you. The breath you need will fill your lungs again. You will be steadied.

Pour. Give. Empty. Love well. This is Whose you are, precious one. And this is my deepest prayer for you. My greatest joy.

I love you.

Love Letter

Inspired by verses in Philippians 3

Dear brothers and sisters, pattern your lives after mine, and learn from those who follow our example. For I have told you often before, and I say it again with tears in my eyes, that there are many whose conduct shows they are really enemies of the cross of Christ. They are headed for destruction. Their god is their appetite, they brag about shameful things, and they think only about this life here on earth. But we are citizens of heaven, where the Lord Jesus Christ lives. And we are eagerly waiting for Him to return as our Savior. Philippians 3:17–20 NLT

Prayer: Today, let me not allow lust to rob me of love — the love I have received and the love I can give. Let thoughts of "what about my needs" and "I deserve" and "literally can't even" be far from me, so that I can hear Your words of "immeasurably more" and "hand-crafted" and "never leave you — ever" so clearly — and let me then speak those words like love letters. Father, please don't let me forget to speak those words. We need those words. We need to be unafraid to speak and and to listen, to stay and to lean close. We need to be unafraid to be a warrior and to be fought for, to sing together, to cry together, to walk together. God, don't let me forget.

I hope you don't mind this little love letter. You know there is no greater delight than to remind you how greatly you are loved. How much I love you. I will tell you every single day, if that's what it takes for you to believe.

Love lets joy spill out and cover the days. Our kind Lord crafted it that way, so that it could not be contained.

How great a love is that?

Be careful of the ones who want to rob you of that joy by telling you love can be boxed and sliced like day-old bread. Don't let anyone pass off outside-in lust for inside-out love. I know, lust is inviting when the days are dragging on and joy's splash is threatened by the flames. It's easy in those moments to allow lust to meander through our minds, picking out pieces of the story that fancy us the privileged or the persecuted and present us as something deserving of different. But this, love, I want you to remember this. Your story begins and ends with Christ. It begins and ends with the incomparable love He has for you. And there is no privilege or persecution that has pen bold enough to bleed through the pages He holds in His hands. If I could wish one wish upon a million shooting stars for you, it would be this one wish — and it's the wish I pray every single day. I want you to know the One who begins and ends your story. I want you to listen as He reads that story to you, I want you to close your eyes and picture every word He speaks. Of nothing becoming something becoming paradise — just for you. Of liberty becoming destruction becoming redemption — just for you. Of life becoming life everlasting — just for you. Of a love so deep and wide that it cannot be contained — just for you.

I love you, and I want that for you. Because that love gives you eyes to see it all as promise and prize — this fragile life and the strength of eternity tucked away like treasure inside it.

No, I'm not there yet either. But every day, I'm listening to that love story. Every day, I'm letting the words take root a little deeper. Every day, I'm falling in love a little more.

And the joy. Every day.

I'm not leaving, love. I'm staying here so you can listen to my story when you would rather not hear your own. I'm staying here so you have someone to read the story to you when you struggle to close your eyes and listen to Christ's voice. He has me here, you know. He let me fall in love with you. He gave me a warrior heart for you. He gave us songs to sing, tears to cry, hopes to hope. He is not letting us go. And His story in us is enduring, transforming us from privileged and persecuted to promise made and never broken.

Crown and Cloak

Inspired by verses in Philippians 4

Finally, brothers and sisters, whatever is true, whatever is noble, whatever is right, whatever is pure, whatever is lovely, whatever is admirable — if anything is excellent or praiseworthy—think about such things. Whatever you have learned or received or heard from me, or seen in me — put it into practice. And the God of peace will be with you. Philippians 4:8–9 ESV

Prayer: King God, beautiful King. You crown us and robe us and set us in Your Kingdom to be peacemakers and songmakers and hopemakers. You find Your great joy in embracing others with our arms, in encouraging others with our words, in caring for others with our lives. Your instruction to us is so simple, so precious. Find joy in the days. Hold the moments out to You, every past and present and future tick on a clock. Be thankful that the ticks are governed by Your very heart — and let Your peace then govern us. Celebrate the things that are good and right and pure and lovely. Always remember that You are so near. You are King of our days forevermore. Lord, help us stand. Please, help us stand.

for you, love ©2017

Beautiful one, I have so much to say to you today. Do you know how greatly loved you are? Oh, how I wish I could find words to describe who you are to me. Perhaps they've not yet been created. Or perhaps God sings them only in His heavenly songs for you. I hear them now.

You are diadem.

You are purple robe.

You are peacemaker, arm around angst, tossing rough moments like stones into rivers to be washed clean and made smooth. You are reminder of the story we are all becoming. Together.

Stand with crown and cloak for Kingdom's glory. Yes, you. Stand.

You are songmaker, harmonies of joy accompanying melodies of grace. Your voice, it keeps singing — the words like feathers on wings of hope. "My great Lord God is here, ever here. Why should I worry and why should I fear? He hears every plea and He holds every tear. Christ's peace captivates me, His love finds me dear."

Stand with crown and cloak for Kingdom's glory. Yes, you. Stand.

You are hopemaker, lifting high what lights life. Hearts turn toward honor and justice, toward innocence and love, toward the tenderness of sacrifice. Oh, what glory there is in lighting life with excellent things. Oh, what peace there is when we let hearts turn toward.

Stand with crown and cloak for Kingdom's glory. Yes, you. Stand.

Watching you now, I am overcome. You have given me strength to stand. You have taught me to find place with your song. And my place is secure. In deepest darkness and in brilliance of noonday, I stand with crown and cloak for Kingdom's glory. For the King calls me beautiful too.

Oh, how I wish the words would find me now, the words of great affection for the kindness you've shown. In moments when I thought I was so very forsaken, God set you there to see me. He saw me in your eyes. He embraced me in your kind arms. He cared for me when you cared for me. And He now lets me do the same. For you.

We will stand with crown and cloak for Kingdom's glory.

Room

Inspired by verses in Colossians 1

He was supreme in the beginning and — leading the resurrection parade — He is supreme in the end. From beginning to end He's there, towering far above everything, everyone. So spacious is He, so roomy, that everything of God finds its proper place in Him without crowding. Not only that, but all the broken and dislocated pieces of the universe—people and things, animals and atoms — get properly fixed and fit together in vibrant harmonies, all because of His death, His blood that poured down from the cross. Colossians 1:18–20 MSG

step inside

Prayer: There is room, even today, even still, for me today. Jesus, You do not move me out or move me into a corner where You do not have to be seen with me. You are room for me when, in protest, I pack my things and say I'm leaving. You are room when I close my own doors and say there is no room in me.

Lord, today I want to celebrate the room I have in You to move and breathe and have place.

Today, I want to see how room in You creates room in me where the invitation lives. "Step inside. Step inside." Today, let me not grow weary when others long or stumble or wonder or wander. Let me not scream over Your voice. Let me not block the way to Your invitation.

In Jesus, there is room **for you, love**. There is plenty of space to stretch wide and find a place where sunlight warms and the fragrance of the breeze is life. Yes, there is room. It is not "Christ makes room" by rearranging the chairs, or "Christ will find room" by inviting you to stand in the entryway. It's "Christ IS room." He is brick and mortar, solid foundation and unblemished glass, windows and doors and the frames that hold them. He is architect and builder, designer and decorator. He is sanctuary and He is sunroom, the place we gather strength and rest and faith. Do you hear His voice? "Step inside. Step inside."

Do you want to see God? Step inside. Christ is room for the longing when you look at the stars and know there is more. Christ is room for the hurting when you question the darkness that seeps through the cracks in the concrete outside. Christ is room for the wondering and the wandering and the waiting. Christ is room. And His voice says, "I see you. Step inside."

He is room to hold you. He is room to keep you.

He Will Not Let Us Fray.

Inspired by verses in Colossians 2

I want them to be encouraged and knit together by strong ties of love. I want them to have complete confidence that they understand God's mysterious plan, which is Christ Himself. In Him lie hidden all the treasures of wisdom and knowledge. I am telling you this so no one will deceive you with well-crafted arguments. For though I am far away from you, my heart is with you. And I rejoice that you are living as you should and that your faith in Christ is strong. Colossians 2:2–5 NLT

Prayer: Today God, please let me see the fullness of color that lives in me, that lives in all You have woven. Father, the threads in me feel so transparent and weak, with pigment bleeding. But I am woven strong. I am all the colors. Every single one. So right now, would Your hands hold the threads that create the design of me — hold them tightly so I can feel Your artisan strength. Restore the colors that are there all along. Thank You that I will not fray — even today I will not fray.

for you, love ©2017

I may never see your face, may never sit beside you on a sofa — cups of coffee in our hands and a box of tissue nearby to wipe the tears. But right now, I want you to close your eyes and see what I see. I see us walking beside each other on this same road, seeing the same glorious light breaking through clouds, feeling the same hope that sometimes is only the slightest glimmer in hearts so very heavy with the weight of this very present life. Yes, I am here and we are woven together like threads in a blanket that offers comfort on some days and warmth on others and always always always color. Brilliant color.

Yes, we are together because Christ has woven us through His love for us, taken our threads and made them roots that go deep, raised them high for all to see.

Our threads are color. Brilliant color. So don't allow monotone shades to wrap around your legs and trip you. Don't allow neutral shades to wrap around your hands and bind you. You are color. You are miraculously woven, powerfully woven, beautifully woven. Every strand in you has been hand-dyed by Christ Himself. He has taken every string of your life and given it life. He has stripped away all that fades and all that wears thin.

So don't let anyone tell you the colors aren't real, that the threads aren't woven well, that the roots aren't deep enough. You need no more than what you are in Christ to be all the colors. When you are told you aren't bright enough, remember Who created you. When you are told your weave isn't beautiful enough, remember who crafted you. He will keep you bright and He will not let you unravel. And He will not let us fray. We are woven together.

I am holding you right now. He will not let us fray.

Look up.

Inspired by verses in Colossians 3

If then you have been raised with Christ, seek the things that are above, where Christ is, seated at the right hand of God. Set your minds on things that are above, not on things that are on earth. For you have died, and your life is hidden with Christ in God. When Christ who is your life appears, then you also will appear with Him in glory. Colossians 3:1–4 ESV

Prayer: Why, God, do I keep looking down? Why do I continue to see myself as slave when You have set me free? Father, let today be the day I no longer grab at chains that You have broken, let today be the day I look up at Love and say, "This — for me." Let today be the day I wear Love and carry Love and speak Love. Oh, to speak Love to a world raped and robbed of its goodness. The tears fall as I imagine what that Love sounds like — could it be the lullaby of a young mother, or the whistle of a grandpa as he tends to orchard trees? Perhaps it sounds like afternoon rain on leaves, or snow under a full moon. Yes, I will look up and wear and carry and speak. Love. Today, I will speak You. This — for me.

Oh, love. Let me look at you. I want to see your face, so lift it. You, precious one, need no longer look down. You have tasted love, so look up and see its source. Love has raised you, and love will carry you now.

Love wants to see your face shine brightly. So look up, look up. No more selling your soul and selling yourself, no more begging and clawing and craving, no more scraping against dirt for scraps of temporary life.

Love wants to see your eyes lit with eternal flame. No more longing looks, no more fearful gazes, no more side glances filled with distrust and deception.

Your face is more now. Your eyes are more now. You are more now. Because you were always more. Always ready to shine. Always ready for fire.

And now love has come. So look up, look up. Precious one, look up.

Look up and see how love wants to adorn you now. He has kindness and compassion and beautiful bearing with others for you. Love has a name — Christ — and He has forgiveness and humble hearts and gentleness for you. Oh, and He has love — His very presence — for you to be worn like a robe. Love is ready to live in and through you now, finding ways to see and words to speak through your trembling lips — words of hope and words of grace and words of merciful strength. Words of always thankful.

For love is always thankful.

Look up, precious one. Look up and see the love that sees you. Let love serve as you serve, honor as you honor, yield as you yield, stand as you stand.

Oh love, let me look at you. You shine.

Dwell.

Inspired by verses in Colossians 4

Devote yourselves to prayer, being watchful and thankful. And pray for us, too, that God may open a door for our message, so that we may proclaim the mystery of Christ, for which I am in chains. Pray that I may proclaim it clearly, as I should. Be wise in the way you act toward outsiders; make the most of every opportunity. Let your conversation be always full of grace, seasoned with salt, so that you may know how to answer everyone. Colossians 4:2–6 NIV

Prayer: There are not enough words of thanks to offer up for the ones who have given time, kind Father. You have built us for belonging, and You are as generous in Your gifts of people as You are generous with the gift of You. Perhaps that's because You delight in revealing Yourself through image and likeness, and Your best miracles are wrought through incarnation. Thank You for the ones kind enough to listen, bold enough to speak, tender enough to embrace, strong enough to carry, brave enough to walk, wise enough to stand, humble enough to pray. Thank You for the ones who are present, no matter where the journey leads. Thank You for the ones who stay, no matter how light or dark the day. Thank You for the ones who dwell.

for you, love ©2017

Our heart comes alive when it feels the heartbeat of another. We are designed to dwell, to sit down and lean back and relax into precious together. So, little love, now is the time to dwell.

Let's be together.

I wish I could be the one sitting with you right now, leaning back and watching your eyes sparkle as we recount story after story of how our belonging to each other may look like a meal or a message or a smile or simple words uttered in quiet rushing moment to moment — but how that belonging is God's own love in flesh and bone, it is His design wrapped in His design.

And yet, we are still together. Time and place have no power over us. Our love is timeless. Our love is boundless. And so, dwell.

Dwell with each other in thankful prayer. Your prayers are the words of a song that echoes throughout eternity, shattering shackles and letting lives soar. Walk with each other, savoring each moment you've been given as one worth sharing. Speak life to each other, mindful of the picture formed by the linking of your words like stained glass.

Listen to those with news to share. Listen in love. Respond with grace.

Welcome those who you meet on the journey. Eyes wide open and arms outstretched, welcome.

Serve those who find their joy in serving others. Comfort and care and wash weary feet.

Dwell in the good news you have received. Invite others to sit and lean and relax. Speak hope, speak truth, speak life. Belong without reservation.

Hold faces in hands and say, "You belong here. You belong well."

Love is timeless. Love is boundless. Be unafraid to share that love. Be unafraid to dwell.

I Want You.

Inspired by verses in Psalm 1

They are like trees growing beside
a stream, trees that produce fruit in
season and always have leaves. Those
people succeed in everything they do.
Psalm 1:3-4 CEV

Today, I want you to walk strong.

I want you to hold the hands of those who
believe you are of great worth, who believe
you have purpose beyond profit. I want
you to stand should-to-shoulder with
those who hold you close and hold you
high. I want you to find your place at the
table with the ones who see meaning
in the days that feel meaningless.

Today, I want you to be strong. I want
you to laugh at the moments before
dawn breaks and the days when
the sun shines brightly. I want you
to be unafraid of the shadows in
valleys so long.

Today, I want you to grow strong.
I want roots to run deep from your
soul to Living Water wellsprings. I
want life to find its place in all you
do, in all you say, in all you give.
You, love, will be planted. You, love,
will grow.

Strong.

50

My Listener

Inspired by verses in Psalm 17

I am praying to you because I know you will answer, O God. Psalm 17:6 NLT

We sit quietly together as the night sky gleams starlight like glitter. You say, "speak love, I'm listening." The room is quiet. You desire nothing but to hear my voice. You say it is music.

We have walked road together, though You smile at that word. For I have not gone gently always by Your side. I have stumbled and faltered, tried to run too fast and refused to move at all. I say we have walked, but You have carried me. You have never let go of my hand, never let me fall from the path.

And so now we sit, and You lean in. "Speak love, I'm listening."

And You catch every word, holding each in Your hands like gemstones. You respond. You smile as the tears stream down Your face. My voice is beautiful to You, my prayers like poetry. I am Your delight. You are my Protector, my Healer, my Listener.

Starlight reflects on gemstone words. You are my Answerer. My Lord.

for you, love ©2017

Speak Love,

I'M Listening.

Sing, my love. Sing.

Inspired by verses in Psalm 40

He has given me a new song to sing, a hymn of praise
to our God. Many will see what He has done and be
amazed. They will put their trust in the Lord. Psalm 40:3

I waited as best I could for the Lord, God All-Mighty. I waited, and He leaned in so very close to me and heard every small cry of my heart. Then He swept me up in His arms and pulled me out of muck and mire that threatened to swallow me alive. He placed me on solid ground — a rock so stable and sturdy. And if that wasn't enough, He gave me a song. He taught me words to a melody I had never sung before. It felt so familiar — like something my soul had heard before and had longed for ever since. He said, "sing my love, sing." And I sang so all could hear. No fear of my pitch or perfection. I just sang the Song. And the words went something like this.

Trust your life to the Lord, and He will entrust Himself to you. Happy are those who don't chase the shadows but find their life in His light. God, Your goodness grows and Your kindness multiplies, and there is nothing that compares to You. As quickly as one story is told, a million new stories are written. You, sweet God are the God of stories that change stories forever.

You, oh God, don't need sparkling wonders to catch Your eye. You don't need eloquent words to entertain You. You, oh God, are the God who says, "just you, my love, just you..."

And so I respond with, "yes — here I am, every good and dark part of me." My joy is to find my joy in You.

I'm singing the song now, humming the tune throughout the day. I've not hidden it, have inscribed the lyrics on my hands. You've written the words of my deliverance. You've written the words of Your faithfulness. You've written the words of the salvation You give and keep giving. And so I sing the love song. I never want to stop singing.

Some days, I sing it to myself, to remind my heart of my soul's security. Because some days my heart is so weary of the darkness it still feels. Some days I simply don't care — some days I simply don't desire. Anything. Nothing.

And yet, You are there, singing the song along with me like a thousand angel voices. You are singing it to remind me that I am forever loved. You are singing it so those who cheer for my demise hear it and turn away.

Oh God, let my song join the songs of the chorus of all who find their hope in You. You have made the nothing of me into beautiful something. You are my help and You are my security. And You will never stop singing to me.

for you, love ©2017

You Are. You Will.

Inspired by verses in Psalm 83

Our God, don't just sit there, silently doing nothing!
Psalm 83:1

I know You are there for me, my God. I know You are there.

Even when the howls of enemy packs echo like wolves in shadowed canyons, when destruction threatens to be etched into souls like carvings on stone, when hope drips from hope like blood on a battlefield, You are there.

And You will rise, God. I know You will rise.

And You will shine.

And all that is broken around us will become radiant stained glass. Howls will become songs of praise. Every piece laid waste will be made whole again. For You are the God of All Things New.

All Things New.

There is no enemy who can stand against You. There is no depth that can't be filled by You. There is no death that can't be raised by Your love.

I know You are there for me. I know You will make All Things New.

56

Celebrate You.

Inspired by verses in Psalm 104

Oh, let me sing to God all my life long, sing hymns to my God as long as I live! Oh, let my song please Him; I'm so pleased to be singing to God. Psalm 104:33-34 MSG

I celebrate You, my King, my Warrior.

Today, I celebrate You.

My heart and my soul hold You high. You are amazing. You wear bright light and glory, and You are majestic and mighty. You stretch out Your hands and heaven becomes my home. You reach out to me, and water becomes walkway. You stand on clouds and ride the wind. You speak and the air becomes Your messenger. I hear Your voice.

You placed earth just so, and then You said, "don't touch her." You painted blue and green and brown upon her like artwork, shifting and shaping until mountains and waterways and plains became perfection. You marked the boundaries with Your finger, and spoke life abundant to creation. Birds found nests, foxes found dens, and man found home. You set the table with food and wine, and invited all to come. You gave strength. You gave gladness.

You crafted days and nights to dance in harmony, and watched as all earth moved in time. Your work is masterful and majestic, intricate and mysterious. Everything finds its place in You, all creation yearns for You. You create, You renew, You redeem, You resurrect.

And You remain.

So I hold You high, O God. I celebrate You now.

for you, love ©2017

If the pages of this responsive prayer journal have inspired you to spend more time with God in reading, reflection, and response, here are a few tips you might enjoy!

READING (from Ronne)

First, to the best of your ability, find a time and space that can become your gathering place. For me, it's first thing in the morning, before I even get out of bed. I have what I need within reach — a notepad, a couple of books filled with prayers, and my laptop. Each night before I go to sleep, I run through the day, thanking God for even the most mundane things — and I pray for the next time we'll commune through the study of scripture. It's a date for me — a precious date that I don't want to miss. I tell people that Christ is life in my veins. It isn't just a poetic statement. My mornings with Him set the tone for the rest of my day.

We are truly blessed with so many translations of scripture, aren't we? I encourage you to read more than one. Some are translated word for word, some thought for thought, and some are paraphrases based on intent and context. Online, both YouVersion (Bible.com) and Bible Gateway (BibleGateway.com) offer parallel views. I'm a Bible Gateway fan myself, because I can view five different translations at once. Three of the translations (MSG, ESV, and NIV) offer audio versions as well, so that I can not only read but hear the Word of God.

I also use Examen.me, a free online Bible study tool that provides a simple guide to studying scripture. It has become one of my best habits, and I thank Brent MInter, its creator, for providing a wonderful way to develop the discipline of prayer and study. I also take advantage of the Notes app on my iPhone, and often copy scriptures that resonate with me into it so I can then add the thoughts those scriptures inspire.

~Ronne

REFLECTION

These books have found their home in our homes.

Valley of Vision: A Collection of Puritan Prayers and Poems by Arthur Bennett
Prayers that read like poetry and dive to the deepest heartfelt joy and pain, this book sits on the nightstands of both Ronne and Courtney.

The Art of Prayer: An Orthodox Anthology by Igumen Chariton
A deep-water drink on the purpose of prayer, and a beautiful look at the Jesus Prayer — the prayer of the heart.

Prayer: Our Deepest Longing by Ronald Rolheiser
A powerfully practical book on the practice of prayer. Ronne has given this book as a gift more times than she can count.

The Only Necessary Thing by Henri Nouwen
The power of prayer is shared through eloquent prose.

The Jesus Storybook Bible by Sally Lloyd-Jones
While written for children, it only takes a few moments reading Psalm 23 or Luke 2 to know that this bible has much to teach adults.

My Utmost for His Highest by Oswald Chambers
How many times does someone need to read Chambers' devotionals before they are no longer pierced to the core? We think perhaps the number hasn't been created.

Thoughts to Make Your Heart Sing by Sally Lloyd-Jones
Free-verse poems inspired by scripture and beautiful illustrations are fuel for Courtney's creative soul.

Tell It Slant by Eugene Peterson
Of course, a book that shares the unique ways Jesus tells story would pique the curiosity of Ronne. She goes back to this book time and time again when she needs a reminder of the power of words well placed.

Hind's Feet on High Places by Hannah Hurnard
Along with Charlotte's Web, this allegory is perhaps one of Ronne's favorite books. She has adventured with Much-Afraid on her journey with the Shepherd so many times.

RESPONSE (from Courtney)

Sterling Publishing Inc. - Sketchbooks in various sizes
These sketchbooks offer high quality paper at a relatively low cost. Even Sharpies don't bleed through, so I feel like I get to use the entire journal rather than every other page. Most sizes come in both spiral and traditionally bound spines, so I can use whichever style works best.

Journaling Bibles -
Ronne and I were talking about how many journaling bibles are being offered these days. I still have my original Crossway bible, with plain black cover and large margins. We both love journaling bibles, whether you are taking notes, doodling, or transforming words into imagery.

Drawing Apps

Paper53

This is one of my favorite ways to journal. The app is easy to use, and has a full library of great tools that come standard. While there are more sophisticated apps out there, like Procreate, Paper53 allows me the opportunity to be fully creative.

Noteshelf

This app allows you to create journals that sit on virtual bookshelves. It gives you the opportunity to customize each journal with the type of paper you want on the inside as well as customize the cover. Again, whether you are taking notes, doodling, or transforming words into images, you'll love Noteshelf.

Pens & Tools

Sharpie Pens

Sharpies were my "go-to" for years. And Sharpie pens are still my favorite for color journaling in my bible. They don't bleed, and they are a great quality at an affordable price. Plus, I like the way they feel on paper.

Paper Mate Flair

These will bleed through bible pages, but for thinline journaling, they are my favorite. They offer rich pigment and many color choices. Plus, they're quite affordable and easy to find.

Steadler Ergosoft Colored Pencils

These are my favorite pencils to use in my bible and for journaling. They are triangular and fit well in your hand. The lead is soft so it blends easily and won't tear the pages of your bible. They come in a at carrying case that makes them easy to take along with you. .

6" Ruler

For sharp underlines and drawing, this has become my new go-to tool, and bonus — it doubles as a bookmark!

Notation regarding Scriptures and Use of Text or Images

Made in the USA
Lexington, KY
11 July 2017